W0081945

Devin's Ink

© 2022 Devin Gossett

Paperback ISBN: 978-1-66785-664-3

eBook ISBN: 978-1-66785-665-0

Devin's Ink

THE SIX PIECES
OF SEVEN

Devin Gossett

Contents

Devin's Seven Volume I - Lost Love

Lovers & Friends

If you and i were lovers

living along the sea being nurtured by nature

unlocking island secrets

with our passion being the key

to be entangled in ecstasy

As we lay in the sand

Two black impressions where

we contorted on the land

if you and i were friends

who ate lunch everyday at 3

by the land tasting and describing

the fuzzy fruit of kiwi

our time spent talking

in lieu of touching

getting lost in each others lip's

instead of being connected

At or compiles at the hips

two meaningful mortals

meeting to mold minds

a friendship is the beginning

to a divine love's design

𝕬 𝖑𝖔𝖘𝖙 𝖑𝖔𝖛𝖊

To see her was to want her

to know her was to love her

to hold her was heaven

what a mistake i made,

to lose her was a tragedy

to mistreat her was a sin

at one times she could have been my love

now she's a forgotten friend

to see her was finding a treasure

today when i saw her i received a gift

seeing her i provided the utmost pleasure

from her presence i received a lift

at one time i was in her thoughts

now i'm just her forgotten friend

now i realize something about her

i've fallen in love with her again.

My Serenade

I cannot carry a note even if cups were glued to my hands

but i would sing to you until i became hoarse

i'd sing every song of love, i love and even the songs

i'd love to be able to sing, just to bring a smile to your face

if dreams were reality and i was able to dream

i'd dream of singing to you from the mountain's top

i'd take a lifetimes fortune and travel to distant lands

learn ancient lunges just to be able

to sing to you in ancient and varied foreign tongue

that would play tantalizing tom-tom beats on your eardrums

i'd sing to you of the love welts and the love for you

that is here to partake of, hold on to and reciprocate thru irrigation

so what we had can sprout again and grow to the heights

and strength of sequoia trees to shadow the light of ur love

from the masses around us for only you and i to enjoy

to you i'd sing a song of forever singing so loudly and powerfully

that Saturn's rings jingle like wind chimes

imitating the melody and frequency of the song my soul hums

and i pray you hear it when the wind blows

because i have stood in the eye of hurricanes and tornadoes

whispering i love you's

between flying fragments, hoping my message gets trapped in the
winds current

3

and reaches you on a sunny day with a light breeze

in lieu of sending you a message in a bottle i'm sending you the song

of my hear that is accompanied by my hearts beat on bass

and the music it makes is sublime but could only be truly divine

if i could sing it to you while holding your hands, delving into your eyes

trying to find the part of me i left with you and hoping you recognize it

praying you accept me and all my faults and strengths

so i'm sing you the song i prepared so long for like a iron chef's famous marinade

if you listen to your heart, i hope you can still hear my serenade.

Without Cause

without cause

she left me today

inside my heart cried

no physical tears rolled down my face

i guess i have to much pride

but inside my heart

it felt as if i had died

to make the best of it

is what i had tried

but despite all my efforts

in the end all i did was sighed

i did everything i could do to please her

at her call i was so quick i flied

in my heart all i wanted was to be with her

to watch the incoming tide

our relationship was a voyage a wonderful journey

i thought a never ending ride

but then she ended it

no reason

no signs

she just ended it today

without care

without cause

The break-up

Harsh were the words uttered from your lips

that you once said to me

you dismissed all hope with an invisible hand

and transformed me into a refugee

depressed and regressed i became sad and lonesome

never again, the same, rearing my head

i might as well have been an outcast to you

easily could have pronounced me dead

my soul you had taken with one fell swoop

like a hawk diving and attacking it's prey

never shall i forget how you unleashed the beast

that came and took my life away.

After You

After you, life is death and words are gasps of breath

an angel you must be the one sent to watch over me

i turned my back to you as if your love was not true

as if your name was, who?

and i didn't know you

now i'm dying and fighting death trying to find answers

yet this cancer is a hermit, alone as the crab

dreaming about the days when you shared my shell

as we shadowed love by the buckets from cupids bottomless well

now i'm stuck as the orator telling the tale of how i failed your love

and above all i miss your breath on my neck when i lay to sleep

i miss catching your tears when you wept with fingertips

now without you mine tear ducts drip, as i am saddened

my days have been blackened as have my dreams

even with cargo pockets full of hope i'm at the end of my rope

as i try to cope with life , i'm falling without you

After you,

who would compare, i'm aware of everything about you

those eyes that pierce me down to the marrow of my bones

a jones, i've developed, that smile has be stretched out for miles

i even howl when i see your profile or a silhouette of your frame

the most angelic name that may sound like the same of other women

but only in an instance from a distance

there is only one like you

no one lit up my life the way you did and still do

so how on earth am i going to go on without you,

what could possibly have meaning

after you

my ears seems to be shattered in halves

and i'm beyond recovery or help

i'm love ill, with the flu, driven by your absence

so alone in my room i'm burning mer and incense reflecting on the
gift of you

you were my life, but now i'm sifting

through the cracks on the concrete

it seems that asphalt is what i taste and soles of feet greet me

the color for sadness has changed from to me from blue

after you.

𝔄𝔡𝔦𝔬𝔰

Even though

i leave you alone today

here my love

for you still stands

i will never forget

the time we spent

on the beach

burying each other in the sand

once more

we go our separate ways

leaving our hearts and love

in the dust

my love for you is strong

but time and distance

make me weak

too far apart

to far away to make things work

to close to cut all ties

its hard to hold

back all these tears

when we are saying

all these good-by's

Devin's Seven Volume VII - My Family Cries and Ties

Memories

Life isn't all strife

Growing up Isn't always enough

What's right isn't the only plight

Yet the reality of death is always tough

If death is just the transfer of energy

I guess, it is really all about the memories

𝔐𝔶 𝔈𝔞𝔯𝔱𝔥, 𝔐𝔬𝔬𝔫 & 𝔰𝔲𝔫

I realized you all are my flowers

I have to shower

Not always every day or every hour

Yet still your time with me now

I devour

In same room or in my presence

You all are my presents

I just want to be there to unwrap your tomorrow

And fight this world to keep you from its

Sorrow

So smile and know you are meant to be wild

Alive and the soil of a tribe to come

Always remember you three

are my earth moon and sun

Heirs

The sins of the father are not the sins of the son's

Yet the regrets of the father can impact their future or outcome

Had I been more aggressive and firm, took action quicker and soon

My constant cloud of gloom caused by distance could have been avoided and the delay for you all to bloom

To be what you can be, even though you are a improved version of me

Better and smarter, in lieu of having a finish line pushed farther and farther because of your father's lack of action

Emotions drove reaction that caused doubt and pain

Never ever did I want to join in the cause for a life of strain, stress or despair

I vow to you all, to turn this around and prepare your rightful thrones for my heirs

For Your Smile

All i do is nothing

but it's something of something

to turn nothing into something with you

You don't know how much my mind flies

when your eyes meet mine in a glance

trapped in time

but i find and i found

peace in your smile

so, the sound of its song

where i stand shakes the ground

all around

It makes my any gesture worthwhile

and you drive me so wild

when you raise your little brow

i don't know how

but i know all that

is a prelude to your smile

You don't know how few words

can explain the pain and the statin i feel

when you are walking away

yet i still feel, it's real

this feeling you peel away and reveal

oh, how i really do love your smile

you don't know

why i do all i do just for you

but you do, and its true

it's all for your smile

Daddy's Mean

Daddy may seem mean sometimes bc I fuss and at times & it feels like it's not fair or you did nothing to deserve it bc you were just having fun.

All I want is the best for you, so you know what's right and what's wrong and one day you will realize it was all for you to be ready when the time comes.

Daddy loves you all with every breath he takes, I'm only trying to guide you the best way I know so you will be smarter than I was at your age.

Don't think for a second that my discipline is to take away your joy. At times daddy hurts too but it's my job to make sure your ready to perform on life's stage

You know you are Gossett's and that makes you just as good as anyone in this world you will ever meet.

Soon you all will be grown and will look back on these days and smile and realize daddy was really a softy and sweet.

My hearts desire is for you to be the smartest people in the room you are in so you will make the best decisions for your lives.

Every day is a lesson so learn from it and take it with you never forgetting when your mad I'm crying inside bc one day I'll lose the queen bees of my tribe.

Anything you ever need I will make sure you have when you need it no matter how old you are

Never will I ever not be there for you never will you not be babies always my guiding stars!

Note to self

I'm here today to tell you to feed your memory right

Just as good as your appetite

Be polite and pure and don't shoot for perfection

Just ensure your only infection is to keep learning

Yearn to increase what you do not know

Show and teach and share, so new leaders are born to grow

Storm through all seasons then do it again

Befriend all and belittle none

For you never know who will be the one,

Who lifts you

Forgive before you forget but never dwell on the past bc you aren't going that way

What has happened, has.

What's to come, is next.

Where you are is the present,

Time is what the gift is,

It is the ability to change as we live.

My Motto

This tree comes

with six seeds of tomorrow.

All have been planted.

My purpose,

my responsibility,

my heart,

my breath.

Now we live.

Devin's Seven
Volume III
Urban Letters

Brainteaser Pt 1

You said sixteen short sentences

each line was poetics in pantomime

i tried to release the squeeze you have on my mind

all my attempts were feeble

your hold on me i can't define

your words captivate me

like the launching of a rocket

every time you walk away

i see my brain stem protruding out of your back pocket

you refill me with terms like a faucet to a tub

you enter my mind as planes to a hub

teasing my brain, remaining like a grass stain

i snort your sounds and verbs like cocaine

even though i can wet you like rain

you continue to cleanse my mind like gain

our written mind games lead me down a one-way lane

i can't get enough of the head pleasing pain

i can feel your poetry throbbing in my veins

how i love the way you tease my brain.

𝔄lphabet 𝔏oue

You keep me full, with your grammar loop food groups

i devour your alphabet soup

licking the bowl

feeding me miracles that replenish my soul

sharing your recipes which are tasty tidbits of your

earthly role

i was told everyone you meet

teaches you one thing or two

i've learned there is no better lesson

than verbally dining with you

your words just flow down my esophagus

and base my stomach acids

they say you never realize your place in this world until

you've passed it

well i've sat and talked to you under gray skies and blue

i caught your vibe like the flu

and consumed your presence as a bowl of beef stew

i've noticed since i first saw you

all i can do is smile at your honey toned hue

oh, how i love to hear you call men boo

now i want to pour you in my glass and do the dew

i have holocaust type list of things you've said that make

me go ooh

now i want to dig in your jar like Winnie the Pooh

when we convert my mind needs to be put in a zoo

you keep me on my toes and on guard like a student of kung -fu

your poetry petrifies my thoughts turning my thoughts to goo

your name clamors in my mind so much

when people say my own, my answer is who

i seem to be attached to your statements as if you have

applied Elmer's glue

and your fragments are just as enjoyable because i like them too

you seem to be a need, essential like a leg joint ligament

I, find myself in a predicament that i can't seem to get out of

simply put, i am enthralled by your alphabet love

Verbal Glue

You have undressed my mind with rhyme

aged my thinking like red wine

i told you together we shine

our exchanges are sublime, time after time

i commit the questionable crime

of turning abstract feelings into physical lyrical lines

it's your picture i paint with my visions

it's not a question of if i listen

easily i intake your words

but it's your presence i'm missing

to be in your favor is all i savor

for you to be in my thoughts is imperative

for knowledge to be sought

i ought to tell you what you do to my thinking

i read your work and feel like i'm sinking

you've driven me to drinking

your liquid words in ink

my eyes no longer blink

i collect your sentences like hard water in a kitchen sink

i drape your rhyme around my shoulders like a mink

still i think

that there is more, more we can learn from each other

no other has inspired like you my lyrical lover

i sneak off in the night to write phrases

that bring delight to your days trying to find the ways

to close the gap i see

between park avenue in Norfolk and Alexandria's road of Janna lee

my thought of us stay sweet like sum made tea, it's a treat

to eat your conversation my imagination runs wild

yet i remain patient

for the hour i can shower you with the touch of my hands

as i recite my heart to you along the sands

i listen to you and hear

orchestra's and bands

i think of you and picture gorgeous paintings

of petite women in oil-based work of Paul Gaugin

to read your words i ran to the lab

to give you a stab with my mental spear

to not have you near is all that i fear

to be out of your reach shard enough almost rough

to try not to check my email is tough

so i faithfully long on to you

stuck i am to you and your verbal glue

𝔅rainteaser 𝔓t 2.

I've been brain teased and mickey slipped a concoction of a
love potion
its effect is rapid heart pumping motion and sends the
notion of lifetime
happiness to the mind,
My brainstem was affected first but this curse
is like no other its side effects are membrane numbing
first the antibodies of my bloodstream searched
for emergency exits to dispose of this injection
but the potions direction was aimed at my heart
now i cannot stand to be apart from this woman
her presence in my life is a necessity she is the best of me
brings it out of me, she said be with me and i chose by
nodding silently
a lifetime with her i could already see, before she asked it
of me she is the model why men study anatomy
i envy her clothes, her bath water and her honesty
all of which confirms her position in my destiny
at first i though the put a root in the form of a love
potion in my blood stream circulation, then i realized
that it was merely her and our conversation that crated
this infinite stimulation where at first i thought she
slipped me a mickey, it was simply her words that gave my mind,

heart an eye's a hickey that would never heal, she has confirmed that she

was un-mistakably real, asked me to peel her from sadness,

the method to my madness was to end her life strain to find happiness that can sustain her, i chose to invade her great cardiac vein to attract her

in fact, prepare her for a life with little to no strife

as my wife, as common said, she is my light and hope

i might be able to be with her if i can continue her dire to

be with me this i plan, to kindle this fire by feeding this campfire flame

so we can remain on the same chord as notes fly from her

vocally inciting and inspiring, mentally and physically and

realistically i am in love, no words can express what she does possess that makes my body wake, just by her thought my body quakes

our chemistry secretes serenity an empty's me of negativity

she said i am her and i can feel and see she is me

the test is for us to believe, we really want to be

no matter what the heavens display to the earth she

remakes my days births rays of sunshine on me,

i still believe this is some sort of love sickness or am i just the victim of this mistress,

either way i love the days she has made this craze for her love potion

just isn't getting any easier oh, how enthralled i am by this beautiful brainteaser

Caught in a glance

You give the galaxy acupuncture with your eyes, healing

the worlds with your glance

by chance i strolled in path of your life of fire

Blinded

now all i desire is bathing you with rhythmic impressions

of poetic perfection

careful with word selection to ensure you catch my silent

suggestions

join me as i skate figure eights on Saturn's rings, sculpting

heart shapes, rings and other

designs to make and mold a memory of me last in your

mind

you are my medication, inebriation by you is easily attained

you are the electrical synapse that triggers sent messages

to & from my brain

i can't conceive the reason why i feel pain when i'm not

around you

you're as beautiful as a blue sky reaches in all 180-360

degrees as you please

easing my lungs when i breathe, being marinated by your

glance manipulated into time for

one more chance to dance with you in the pale moonlight

simply to catch you bring day to night

Plus, i love the way you lift and lighten my worries, so i

run jump jog and scurry to feel the

feel the flurry like chills you send and play on my spinal

chords

like a ford i want to explore more of you until we can,

escape away on matching

mustangs, as i escort you to a sight where can lay and

connect the dots to the constellations

in the sky as I recite lyrics of love and light, similar to a

string-less kite

i'm floating above clouds dodging bolts of lightning to get a

view of you during its strike

angels don't dwell in this concrete and grass land nor do

they recognize the average man

yet i see through my third eye so i recognize gods when they

walk and fly by

i'm traveling the trail looking for paths less taken, that

glance has my soul shaken

raking my thoughts to recall what blessings brought you

my way

where are you today will we grow gray

beauty that defies gravity raised me to inner heights,

radiating like suns fir's light

enlightening and brightening the world, curl up and hurl

these previously unheard words

their written on this thin striped college ruled white girl

Calling earl, regurgitating verses exclaiming in which

way that face curses the sense of sight

this night as every other, mind smothered chunked and

covered with you in lieu

of sharing my thoughts, i've prepared an alphabet stew

for you to dine, snack & chew

you make the sun jealous when you arise in the morn, the

heavens as i are torn

not knowing when days ends when around you as you are

the brightest star

bringing light to the night, until you rest wherever you

go you glow

letters are blessed when you speak them, eyes are cherished

when they behold your vision

Your impression leaves burned silhouettes on retina's

Reminding the eyes that all other visions are lies, & I despise

lies cries

yet wise enough to know the only truth is the memory of

the reflection in my mind's eye

so now i'm blind with you, and the bells are chiming as

they did for us

sick form the love bug that bit me, burned me basically

bellowing a sirens song along the beat

of my heartbeat, that skips as i hear your melodiously

molding voice notes that make mine

eyes drip with tears rolling down cheeks to my lips, still

stuck on that smile, it's my only

thought, stuck in this spider's web i'm trapped and caught

Devin's Seven Volume IV - Mr. Libretto

She's not my wife

She's not my wife

But if she were, I'd drape her in the finest fir and silk

Unless she was against it

I'd bather her in milk, honey and lotion her with love to moisturize her

Clothe her with affection and offer her my ears to speak or sing to

When she speaks it seems like, Stevie wonder singing these three words

I'd love to love her die to have her yet no matter how absurd it sounds

She's not my wife

If she were, I'd recite the words I write at night to her by the moonlight

At daybreak, i'd freestyle the way the morning blesses her skin

I'd awake right before she just to see her open her eyes to smile at me

Morning breath and all I'd await my morning kiss immediately to get through my day at work

Can't wait to get back home to her to ask, how was her day?

As I removed her shoes, rubbed her feet after greeting her with a gentle kiss to my cheek and I'd do this every day if I had my way yet

She's not my wife

She's the definition of beauty, an example of class, her walk, her voice, those eyes

I find myself making faces anytime I'm graced by her presence in any place when she crosses my path

I find myself growing in her gaze and balance and memory of our last conversation

Her vision has me pacing at times but,

She's not my wife

I have to tell myself this when I see her and when she walks away

Yet, when we converse I see everything I've ever wanted

In her I see everything I ever needed

I hear the angelic voice I want to hear wake me

Never felt her touch physically but her eyes have pierced me

Her smile warms me in a place I call my dreams

I have gotten the pleasure to learn a little about her and now I yearn to learn more

When she is around me time stops

Nothing matters for a moment in time, at a time she gives me her attention and I feel like she wanted to

But

She's not my wife

She isn't my wife, she's my friend and even though hidden

Feelings I have will never reveal themselves

As I have too much respect for her and more than she will ever know

I'd never disrespect her and ruin what little I do have with her

She's someone I can always confide in, walk with and outline the characteristics of a love I await for in life

I'd love if I could find someone similar to her but unfortunately

She's not my wife

What I needed

I need to see the sea

With you

Be on the sea and sand

Really Just need my bland

That's full of flavor

My neighbor of choice

And voice I yearn to hear

That removes fear of tomorrow's

Pain that's waiting to greet me

Your presence is the present that

I can't get enough of unwrapping

With you it's never any acting

It's the realest phase of me

The energy is always replenishing

Forgiving of no fault

Foundational as asphalt

To build on and with

Simply a gift that's received over and over again

First a friend that loves like a lover

Covering me with exactly what I need

The garden of seeds

That feeds and nourishes

Desires and hours and sprouts flowers

Of dreams I never knew I could conceive

Making me believe that I can achieve

With positivity that's so genuine

I can't believe I'm actually

Hearing it voiced and spoken

Which makes this broken body

Feel whole again

Enough to dare to start again

Filling hope in an empty aqueduct

Where trust used to flow

Showing me tomorrow

That I don't know will be there

But providing one I can dream about

Spouting fresh-water wells of love

Above the thoughts and trials of yesterday's pain

Nameless formless shapeless

Just love

Above my darkness

Heart filled in lieu of a

Heartless past

At last I can think of a future

Like a surgeon with a suture

Sewing me together

With a quilled feathered pen, I begin

To end yesterday bc I'm not going that way

And you provide light

In darkest light

Restoring what's right in the world

My maiden my heartbeat

What I needed was . . .

Sorry

I'm sorry,

Sorry as a SOS never answered

Sorrier than the man that didn't respond to it

I'm sorry,

The same sorry ass that has selfishly made women aware

They are not the only one

Yet still made each feel that way

For that,

I'm sorry,

I can apologize a hundred thousand times, multiple times

ten

Make a million, write 500,000 I'm sorry and still be sorry

500,000 more times

Yet I wouldn't blame any of you for not accepting any of

my apologies

I'm sorry that I've bowed my head, bent elbows and knees

With arm, leg, leg arm and head to beg and plead I my

prayers for forgiveness for hurting all of you

So, I'm writing how sorry I am on paper with ink

So I can read it to myself, and rise out of this hole of guilt I

sink and lie in

I've shredded feelings, burnt emotions, defecated on tears

that smeared make up

Then made the sweetest statements on ear lobes the second

they needed to be heard

That made women dream up fairytales to please me daily

The way I like, only to make them wake up one day to see,

I'm sorry.

I'm sorry you love me, sorry you loved me

Put trust in me, supported me confided, cared and made

Thick "karo" syrup like Love to me

I only reciprocated stress, hurt, betrayal and disrespect

Rejecting your heart and its feelings only providing

Deception at the start to catch you in the web of my

personality

And you were love ing me, every inch of me, every follicle

on me, every scent of me, giving forever and infinite love

for me

that could be seen, touched and smelled

Any observer could taste it by a glance of us together

I still cheated and pilfered loving from other women

Gave away kisses, the ones your eyes told me you missed and

longed for

So I now stand here not apologizing because

I'm sorry.

My Music

The music my mandrakes drowns out the world

When I curl up with speakers and microphones

As melodies are made from the poetic parade

Of these phrases that match the tone of the speaker's moan

My every third line drowns out sound as wine to a meal

Peel back my exterior to find the real music that lies

within

Behind the bones that cover my mental

I use pens, paintbrushes, crayons, markers and pencils

To create the lyrics to the song of my life

The music my mind makes invades mind waves

Ending up on radios, compact discs and tape decks

That can be heard when I frequent clubs and make

speakers pop

My music is jazz, blues, heavy metal, country and hip hop

What I drop on eardrums beats and heats

Creating adrenaline gland to drip and leak

My music plays with emotions as a massage does with an

experienced touch

and lotion

You can call my music an erotic potion

If the word play is turned up to four for fornication

I try to keep my lyrical conversation on a higher level

than physical manipulation

Hear the words but feel the message in the music

Understand the statements but listen

Lips move but the voice is the tool that plays ear drums and

fondles emotion even in the midst of commotion

Souls can be soothed, and people are then moved

By what visions their eyes freeze

Please don't misunderstand the messenger because the

Message is crystal clear as a shallow fresh-water lake

That never ripples, this world is a jar and this poet is the

pickle

That tantalizes taste buds and eyes and removes the disguise

From lies told over waves of sound

I boldly remove the lid drink of this life juice

And sing lines that boost the should and mind state

My music leaves memories behind as a keep sake that are

sung season round

These rhythmic lines were created by design

Simply meant for the listener to enjoy the sound of

My music.

When J used to write & When J used to run

I used to write

I used to run

I used to write and write until what I wrote when spoken

Grew feet and walked away

Carrying words as leaved seeds in the wind

I used to write

I used to write, until day became night then id stop writing and run into the night until I met dean and id begin again to write

I used to run

I used run, until my shoes soles were shaven slices of Swiss cheese full of holes exposing my bare foot

I used to run

I used to run to write for miles until states were crossed and coasts covered

My pencil ran with me and together we speared so and so's across a nation when I used to run

I used to run to write and sometimes write while running

Attempting to catch the tale of inspiration as it flew in front of me

I used to write of running on the moon's surface, praying I could find my souls reflection

In the night of space since I've never seen it during the days when I used to run and write in the day light

I used to write

I used to run

I used to write and write until my pencil's point and eraser were an inch apart

I used to write until pens went dry and only could be used to impress paper pages or loose-leaf books with no spiral loops or hardbacks

I used to write of affection, illusion, memories and confusion

I wrote of intoxication, delusion, omnipresence and seclusion

Sal nation and satisfaction

I used to write

I used to write despite the fact it costs to have a future

I used to write despite the odds

I used to write, I used to run

I used to run because I am an American black male

Use duo run to ignorance in lieu of running into the light

I used to repeatedly run to wrong instead of running right

I used to run

I used write,

I used to write of the light I wanted to run to

And one day I ran into that light saw what was right

Picked up a pad and pen and began to write

I used to write day, night morning, noon the next day and next night just to write

I used to write of running then I sat to write

Still writing of when I used to run

Still writing today and will continue to write as its all I do and as long as the sky mirror seas shade of blue

Writing of what happened in-between those shadows of what is mystical and true is what I shall do

So, I will continue to write of what I used to

when I used to run and write

Her Name

She's too fine for me

i don't believe she won't hurt me

every ounce of life in me desires to try

her eyes hide no lies to me, if they do it's not a thought or

concern

her welfare is my wellbeing and if she smiles i smile

if she is happy i'm content and only if she frowns will i cry

the world i can afford and i would lather her with

my salary, to bestow to her care for her and i without

question

would love to try, to be the man in her life, a man she can

lean on, depend on and count

the seconds of her life with, i count the seconds she allows

me to remain in her presence

ticking at every minute like a service tone reminder on a

cell phone

i've been alone and that way can remain, yet if an

opportunity ever arose

to be close enough to be the thorn on her rose

she can prick me and prune my bad habits away and

release the best in me

i've only been a friend to her, two ears to lend tow hands

to assist

to feet to meet and two laps to respond to her wishes but

never kiss she's too fine for me.

When i was able to jump and scurry with gifts and lifts of

sweet and kind words

absurd it would be, to destroy what little we do share, i

care for her

that line i'd never cross but in the back of my mind

i'd age with her like wine, sign her name on myself

in the location of her choice just to ask in the aroma of

her laugh when she reads it

it's like any discomfort she feels makes my life seem real,

my all would go into her spring, summer and fall to

catch the leaves that fall

before she steps, just to be part of some second inter destiny so

she's comfortable

the world of her i think and in a blink i still tell my self

she's too fine for me

too fine of a lady, to fine of a woman to fine of person

to waste time on or with a man who has not been faithful

this decade

only grateful enough to give kind hello's to

small conversation should be the only invitation she

should offer

to man like me, a peasant, a pauper, who has no real to

look

in royalty's direction and never ever say,

her name

Mr. Libretto Slams

With the hand of the sphinx I slam

Scribbling silicon samples to show the sapience

My satire is slapdash causing scandal leaving scars

On scriptures

I scalp cub scouts simply to screw with and scramble sciences, my script seizes spice and seeks out secrecy

One day my spirit spoke and so I started sprinkling

Stander-by's with sound that sedates spinal chords

Sending schismatic shudder through you like sperm flagella

My spasmodic lyrical scotch is sour to the souls that can't savor the sonnets I scoured ears with

Sparking synapses in your mental stencil

The combination of staccato slang is a stimulant that stings ya stomach up to the sternum

My world is a sphere and I'm here

A spendthrift who scopes then scoops the knowledge of stoics

Then schedule the sky to give clouds spams so the sun shines

My common sense must be on stilts

When I scheme, I smother what the stars cover even on starless nights

I'm the one who steers students the right way

Of the great orators I'm the soothsayer

Lyrically lacing love through the world with lengthy librettos

Like a smile I describe the world with lavish letters that link language

So, others can learn from the life I'm living

It's likely that those who listen to the logic I'm launching

Are located in the area that I look upon

My lines leave legacy that lists the so called, leaders

Locally to London

I lead and recite words of lead that touch the lowest

Classes in life

I know little of much and a whole lot of nothing

My latest revelations that I belong in a land where lyricist lounge and leave legacies on empty lots

Lifting all who hear and understand these lines on a attitude where the mind accepts lessons

Large enough to burn believes like lava over land

I let loose this lip labor and lasso little ones

Letting them know that there are no such things as lock ness monsters and leprechauns

My lassies faire attitude is informing the masses that stealing knowledge is not larceny

But to latch on to a lie is a leach on a corpse in a Lukewarm lake

Abandoning amateurs who lack the academic aptitude to achieve autonomy over their lives

I use an ax to leave these ass-backward individuals minds ajar

So oxygen can reach their brain ,and automatically trigger an avalanche of common sense to set an alarm off to these any bodies

Out of the abyss of achieving nothing

In an album I'm going to begin the amalgamation of this nation

Arbitrate with any who stand ahead in the way of an affordable academy

I'm the acting antibody attacking this virus that is destroying men women and children

I'm allowing all to join this affair as I pass out announcements and post advertisers on aqueducts

Airstrips in airtight auditoriums as I speak apathetically

To audiences offering the knowledge I've amassed as a gift from an Ariel view

The aisle between the alumni can be seen even on autumn auburn nights

Making a human mosaic from the mixture of the many people in motion

My message cuts like a machete through metal or mortar

My mind is magnetic attracting like minds over mountains and
Through meadows

My mentor molded me into a medley making machine

Free of malarkey and meager messages even when I moan

There is a moral

What I've become is a mellow mobile member of mercenaries who
mosey to the sound of a different drummer's music

Mentally I'm immortal mesmerizing the masses with

Machiavelian philosophy, made to murder weak minds

Compared to ordinary mammals I'm mammoth

If the average person reciting poetry is hot

Then I am magma

Melting all who are measuring my alphabetic mesh

Yet merciful so I don't murder, I maim

Making magic to crus these average poetical maggots

I am Mr. Libretto

Devin's Seven Volume V - For The People

Third Class Treatment

As i sat beside my mother, i heard all the talk

they criticized the way we dressed, even we way we talk

and walked

they didn't want us to be here on the same carriage as they

all we could do was endure the pain and pray for a

better day

they turned at us and pointed some even shouted out names

but my mother and i just embraced each other as sat there

being shamed

why were we the target of all this hate

all we wanted was a ride to our front gate

i wish i could understand the people of this world

i wish i could show them even a pebble if polished

can turn out to be a pearl

My Brother

his weight will never tire me

for we shall never be apart

he will never be to heavy

because i lift with my heart

i will lift him from the darkness

like i've been done by another

his weight will never tire me

he is my brother

i will lift him from these stereotypes

America has put him in

i don' see those labels

as i look at him from within

i will lift him from this earthly materialist plateau

where all life's evils dwell

place him in a utopia

where our father will say all is well

then one glorious day on this higher plate

he will see another

and he shall lift up another young soul

warming him with his love

out of love for his brother

This woman

I know this woman

fabric lays atop her and she enhances it

she receives more than the average glances

these women are gorgeous but aren't they all

as plentiful as leaves in the fall

i've fell for this black woman

she is the core to life that's why i'm taking applications

for the wife to be and a black woman is mandatory

If you want to make love, she is the recipe

treat this woman better than she treats herself

that is her due and destiny

I'm going to give her the best that i got

like Anita, because that is what's best for eternity

this is what can be done to honor her majesty

sometimes this woman isn't aware that she will be what she

shows me, i will always be there to have her back

she comes in so many shades and flavors of choice

when she passes by, she eclipses the sun leaving those shaded in

the dark as she strolls, she is a sister, an aunt, a daughter a mother
and friend

she sends me, Sam cooked up a ballad about her personality

gradually she has driven me to see that she was made for

me and I her, even though we are only a blur in her visions

men have hurt her and discarded her

not showing her the attention, appreciate and dedication

she deserves, society tells her good a good black man is a book on

reserve that's always cheeked out yet i still praise her from head to toe

as every black woman i've encountered has helped me grow

stand by this intoxicating woman's eyes lips hips and hue

her arm, leg, leg arm and head leave my eyes red, speech

slurred with my senses weak and roaming

there is nothing like her, this beautiful, black woman

An 𝔥𝔅𝔈𝔘

day in day out

BLACK-ality

from Monday through Sunday

BLACK-ality

these institutions of unreality

are faded to black

with a permanent shade

the days are broken into hours

around the world there is a Godiva haze

that envelops every novice

a pound of pride

you can detect in every student

who has been here and gone

and we live in this BLACK-ality

from each sunset to each delightful dawn

lifelong friendships here are made

and those who come here lost

can leave here saved

here we live inside

this chocolate world

creating and cultivating our minds

polishing these perfect Tahitian pearls of poetry

as we watch the passing time

here in BLACK-ality

holidays are breaks

and breaks are rare to receive

here we get tested on everything

from our speech to what we believe

time has no meaning in BLACK-ality

nor does age here we grow and ripen

some call their reality a cage

BLACK-ality

can be found across the origin of this nation

our historically black colleges and universities are the

places we need to go to solidify our rule

here when we learn from each other we truly identify

how to use our god given tools

Fortified Fingers of Five

There is a method to my madness if you listen to the

messenger

my dream can be reality, actually it's our dream

it seems we don't see it or don't believe it

right now, we can't even conceive it

does it take chains of steel to show disbelieving eyes the

struggle is real

people peel a banana but dispose of the truth

we eat the Baby Ruth because it is said to be tasty

but can you race me to the library

that's a statement we never say, our minds are like a cup

i pour knowledge in mine

i'm offering those who read this a sip

i want you to taste that we are running out of time

i want you to sweat truth, and knowledge of ourselves

so, we can survive

our unity is like a fist

the fortified fingers of five

our strength is just like these fingers of five

if we could come tighter like that fist

our tribe will rise, survive and remain alive

this fist signifies the power we possess when unity is on our

minds

dreams of unity should never rest, and we are running out

of time

our woman, are alone or hungry for material things

not realign what worth, confidence, love and respect they

bring our men are gone either in streets, on drugs or iron bars

are what they cling

while phrases disrespect ring throughout the songs we sing

time is short so we must act now

unify while we can while we can re-learn how

every black man is your brother every black woman that

better half or better side

striving to be better people for each other will be our

guide

if groups of five fortify our truth will destroy their lies

if groups of five unify our hope turns into battle cries

does it take being punched in the fact to open your eyes

are you going to allow your sister to be killed, raped, stabbed

or another mother to cry consume and carry this message on

put a death to our division with a kiss

our power and our unity are in the palm of our fist

The Night

Go out into the night

search for unseen and unheard

flirt with dreams but be at peace with reality

seek out that moon that shines somewhere

sing of the sun to come to bring back that moon

go out into the night

go back and study his story and see tomorrow

rewrite it and guide your own path today

go to the night till light finds you

blinds you and binds the bond between you and the moon

go out into the night

the night revives you rests you cares and flies and invites
you

entices brightness and shades you the night lays on you and
never crushes you

yet brushes you with balance to life's nights and days

go out into the night

the day has clouds and clear skies, yet the night keeps stars

that shines bright from earth and moons away

like stars, balls of energy we are, and we too shine

when we go out into the night

the night absorbs envelopes and surround you

silence echoes and awaits you

sprays, says and defecates days for you

yet is taken for granted, go out into the night

Love into the night, until moons disappear and sunrises

become noon's

Till sunsets to moons and allows love to mushroom into

years and ages

allowing love to grow and grow until it has many nights

that have passed

love into the night and fall in for the first time

at the end of every day and love that love every night

go out into the night

Learn of the yesterday, today and tomorrow and fill the

hollow void in yourself

never stop learning because you must

every night that passes is a new night, gather hunt and

steal all you can learn

till a yearn for the next night to learn haunts you, learn

of yourself as ever night falls

go out into that night

Live like life, lives only once and live like there are no

more nights

No more tomorrow s to follow tonight and live

go out into the night

Dream of a Racist-Less Society

I know tomorrow is unseen but i know what is there,

somewhere a sun is shining beaming and blinding the land

of woman and man

the land of trees and beast a food chain in motion with

racism still present

as minerals and elements like the sediment racism remains

as a stain

or pain the mere thought i can't sustain as it burns cells in

my brain when anyone bears

the name of racism

minds are enclosed in prisms walking in this world

teaching and deceiving

children, young boys and girls are being fed the lies that

disguise and blind eyes

from the cries i loudly cry for racism to stop

it's as brutal as a cop billy clubbing a man the block on

routine license check

a step from snapping this man's neck over his check for

nor reason

the man, just happen to fall in the fold and fit the cold

clay mold

of having a visible soul that was at one time sold as gold

it's everywhere i go and everywhere i turn it burns my

retina when i plain daylight

when radio waves carry the disease my heart ignites

urging my fortified fingers of five to strike

to make a fist and fight and enforcing what is right

despite the risk

i write the plight on paper with stripes and bleed my gripes

racism is real, uncut and still obscene as it stays dry in

precipitating weather, cool and wet when it's so hot

oxygen is severed from your heart for years

it has driven mankind a nation and families apart

now racism can be found searching business suits

Kenneth Cole or Rock-port boots in lie of white sheets

now racism baby sits children and raise them to work in

cahoots with radical factions and organizations it is slowly destroying

the nation but the real question is why?

How can you hate yourself and call yourself in good

health

no matter the facet here is but one race we are humans so

disregard all the summing

and fine tune your thinking, i'm blinking and drinking

this hate juice and can't digest it

I speak my mind and end up arrested but i'm blessed, so I get

rid of all ill feelings

like banana peelings i'm constantly reeling in love so I

deal with lost individuals

attempting to guide or assist, trying to keep an open arm to

love a racist

Devin's Seven Volume VI - The Muse in the Moment

Little did she know

How these conversations

And simple small talk

Have walked around my mind

across these seconds hours and days

It's amazing how photos mutually favored

Creates a desire similar to Lays potato chips

As I can't have just one

Cordial contact and exchanges

Have my phalanges tingling to text

So what's next but to arrange a location

Where we can take these words and allow them to

introduce eyes to dance, hands to shake prior to

pulling up seats to meet, greet and treat each other with presence

It's your time that's the present

I await the opportunity to unwrap the gift of your heart

as that's where I prefer to start

With the hope that one day when we depart

you will think of me and yearn to learn more while apart

maybe I'm a dreamer, just a hopeless romantic who believes that
souls never grow cold when love is a possibility

Or

Maybe I am all that and maybe just maybe

One day that dream transforms into a reality

Mirror

How do you not see what I speak of when you look at your reflection

Should I take ballots of those I know that have seen you for an election of the masses to convince you of your beauty

It's truly a rare occurrence in nature when naturally you possess what others pay to paint and create

Using faces as a canvas to convince themselves of their god given splendor to find comfort in the art they create

When all you have to do is roll over and rock the Brave hair and stun on any interaction

With little to no action other than to smile those rose pedal flavored lips

Maybe if you taught me the phrases to spit in Hindi or Punjabi my point would be made clear enough for you to find the confirmation

In my displayed elation of how beautiful you really are.

I guess I have to fly across the world and trek the Himalayas through a windy blizzard

Just so you can see that faces introspection out of an iced carved hand held mirror.

You

You could have warned me about those eyes

Yet I failed to realize, So much more

The curve of those lips

That profile the thought of those hips

In my dreams are the stuff of legend and folklore

Adore you I do, I don't have enough letters

To combine that can speak to the wine

You pour into me in our conversations

Not just inebriation,It is also elation I feel

like fire in darkness

You finesse me with simply how you talk

The memory of your walk

Is outlined in chalk the vision

Is laced in my mind

All I want is the time that we can align

So I stand I can, close enough to grab you

Pull you close enough to hold and feel your heart beating on my chest

Till our cheeks rest face to face

Just to slide across cheeks until we face

Eye to eye as lips slip together to press

Sunset

From the he breaking of the dawn

To the stretch and yawn after eye lids crack

I wonder if I cross your mind

Time never felt as slow as when we were exchanging nouns adjectives and verbs just hours ago that didn't even feel like night time

Conversation that collided states erasing distance, that felt like we were in an adjoining room getting lost in each other's eyes

As the sun sneaked in my window this morning I realized that I was dreaming and that the light I saw was your smile that mortal men call the sunrise

Even though I know that destiny is a fickle thing that's misunderstood and placing all eggs in one basket isn't a safe bet

I'd empty the bank and go from Atlantic City to Las Vegas to gamble if the prize was a chance to see that face light up the night sky at sunset

Memories

Life isn't all strife

Growing up Isn't always enough

What's right isn't the only plight

Yet the reality of death is always tough

If death is just the transfer of energy

I guess, it is really all about the memories

Friends First

An open nose Tends to run

And the hesitation of allowing love in

Again is a maybe

Maybe another chance to play and prance,

Is a temptation that desires conversation

To feel The feeling of elation is too much to bear

Which leads at times a soul to become bare too soon

As a cancer I turn to the moon to dictate the right phase

To guide the appropriate phrases to speak

Weak from lost love, being hurt from last love

drives apprehension to love once more

Adore I do the thought of a you

That could possibly quench this thirst

But first a promise to be honest and true

Must be proven for gates to open

So new love can again flow through

Time I can't control but today I can try

To make intentions known and to be understood

Today I stand only as a man who knows that he can

Once more to begin and to give his all to first a friend